HOW DOES
IT GROW?

FROG

Jinny Johnson

Illustrations by Graham Rosewarne

FRANKLIN WATTS
LONDON•SYDNEY

An Appleseed Editions book

First published in 2009 by Franklin Watts
338 Euston Road, London NW1 3BH

Franklin Watts Australia
Hachette Children's Books
Level 17/207 Kent St, Sydney, NSW 2000

© 2009 Appleseed Editions

Created by Appleseed Editions Ltd,
Well House, Friars Hill, Guestling,
East Sussex TN35 4ET

Designed by Helen James
Edited by Mary-Jane Wilkins
Picture research by Su Alexander

ISBN 978 07496 8787 8

Dewey Classification: 597.8' 9

A CIP catalogue for this book is available from the British Library.

Photograph acknowledgements
page 5 Keith Ringland/Photolibrary Group; 17 David M Dennis/
Photolibrary Group; 19 Paul Franklin/Photolibrary Group;
29 Michael Leach/Photolibrary Group
Front cover Paul Franklin/Photolibrary Group

Printed in China

Franklin Watts is a division of Hachette Children's Books,
an Hachette UK company.
www.hachette.co.uk

Contents

Laying eggs

Frogs are very happy **living on land** or **in water**. But a frog's life nearly always **starts in water**.

A frog mum lays **lots of eggs**, sometimes hundreds of them, in a pond. The eggs are inside **clumps of clear jelly**, which helps to keep them safe. Other animals like to **eat** frog eggs.

The frog eggs are called **frogspawn**. Can you see the little **black specks** in the jelly? These are the beginnings of baby frogs.

What does the baby frog look like?

A tiny tadpole

At first a **baby frog** looks nothing like its parents. It hatches as a tiny swimming creature called a tadpole. A **tadpole** has a **rounded body** and **a long tail**.

When the tadpoles hatch they **eat the jelly** around them. They are small and weak at first and stay together, **clinging to water plants**.

Tadpoles have **feathery** strands on their heads called **gills**. Gills help the tadpoles **breathe in water**.

Can you see the feathery gills that help the tadpoles breathe?

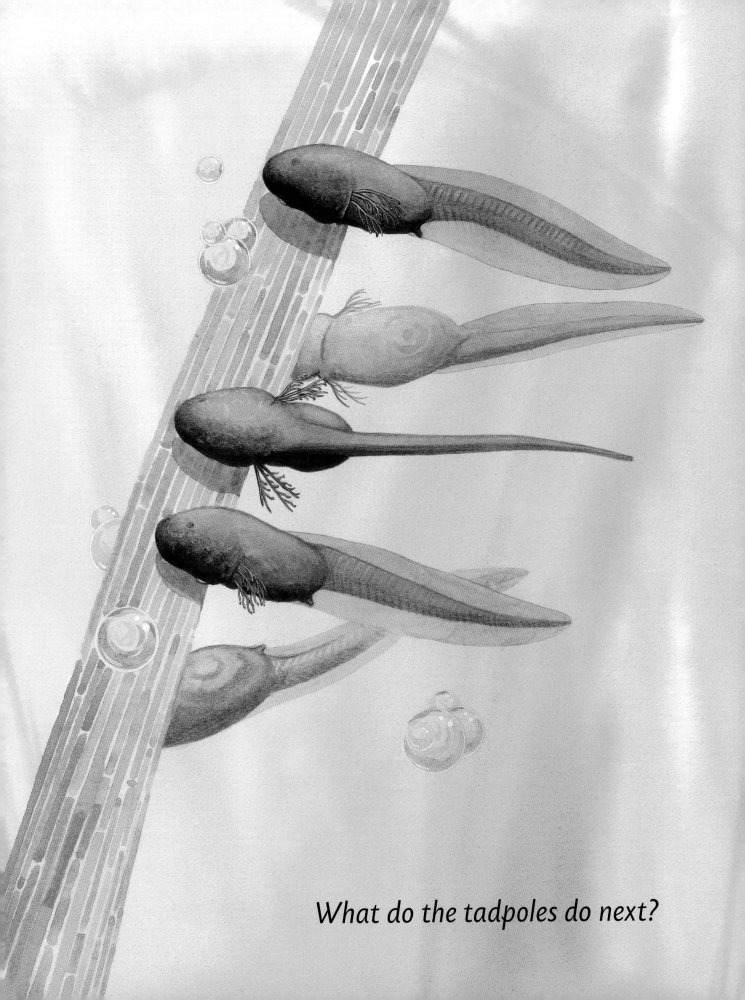

What do the tadpoles do next?

Getting bigger

A week or so **after hatching** the tadpoles have grown bigger. They swim around with the help of their **long tails**, and **feed on water plants** and other tiny bits of food.

Fish and birds eat lots of tadpoles, but some manage to stay safe and survive.

Gradually the tadpole's feathery **gills disappear**. Its **lungs** start to grow and it comes to the surface of the water **to breathe**.

When does the tadpole grow legs?

Growing legs

The tadpole's legs begin to sprout when it is between **six and nine weeks old**.

The back legs grow first and the **tail** starts to get **smaller**.

You can see **bulges** on the tadpole's body where the **front legs will grow**.

Now the tadpole is beginning to look more like a frog.

10

What happens next?

Becoming a frog

By the time it is **eleven weeks old**, the tadpole has grown **front legs** as well as back legs.

Its tail is starting to disappear and it looks more **like a tiny version** of its mum.

Now it **catches insects** to eat, as well as **eating plants**. Soon it will be able to **leave the water**.

THE TADPOLE
HAS FOUR LEGS.

How will the little frog move on land?

On to dry land

Now the **froglet** has grown
bigger it can hop about on land.
Its **tail has gone** and its legs
are **growing stronger**.

The frog's back legs are much
longer than its front ones and
help the **frog jump** into the air.

The frog is **big enough** to catch
lots of different kinds of food.
It likes to eat **snails, slugs and
worms**, as well as **insects**.

How does
a frog catch
its food?

Catching a meal

A frog catches food with its **long sticky tongue**.

Frogs can see well with their **big bulging eyes**. When a frog spots its **prey** it goes as **close** as it can.

Then it jumps towards the prey and **flicks out its long tongue**. The **sticky tip** of the tongue **traps the prey** and whisks it into the frog's mouth in the blink of an eye.

THIS FROG IS
GOBBLING UP
A GRASSHOPPER.

Can frogs swim as well as jump?

Swimming and diving

Frogs are **good swimmers**.
Their feet have **skin between
the toes** that helps them
paddle along. They are called
webbed feet.

A frog has **four toes** on its front
feet and **five** on its back feet.

Frogs spend lots of time
on land but like to stay
near water. They can
dive into the water
to escape from
animals such as
hungry birds.

Why do frogs like to stay near water?

A frog's skin

Frogs like to be **near water** to keep their skin damp. A **frog's skin** lets **water in and out** – so frogs 'drink' through their skin.

Frogs can **breathe through their skin**, as well as with their lungs.

Frogs can't keep their bodies warm so they have to sit in the sun to **warm up**. To cool down they hide in **a shady spot**.

Many frogs can make their skin **lighter or darker** to help them **soak up** more or less **heat**.

When do frogs have
young of their own?

Calling to a mate

When a female frog is **two or three** years old it starts to look for a mate so it can **lay eggs**.

Male frogs **croak** to let female frogs know they are around. **Sacs of skin** under the **chin** fill with air when the **frog calls**. This helps to make the croaking sound **louder**.

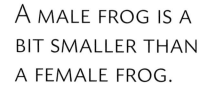

A MALE FROG IS A BIT SMALLER THAN A FEMALE FROG.

Do females croak too?

Female frogs

Female frogs don't usually **croak**,
but they can hear the **male's songs**.

A female frog **knows** how to
recognize the calls of frogs
of **her own kind**.

Frogs' ears are **flat and round**.
You can see them on either side
of the frog's head.

FROGS OFTEN
CALL TO THEIR
MATES AT NIGHT.

What happens when a frog lays eggs?

Starting again

When the **female frog** is ready to lay her eggs she goes to the water.

As she **lays her eggs**, her mate holds on to her. He **fertilizes the eggs** in the water.

Soon lots of **tapoles** will be swimming in the water and some of them will grow into frogs.

A FEMALE FROG LAYS THOUSANDS OF EGGS.

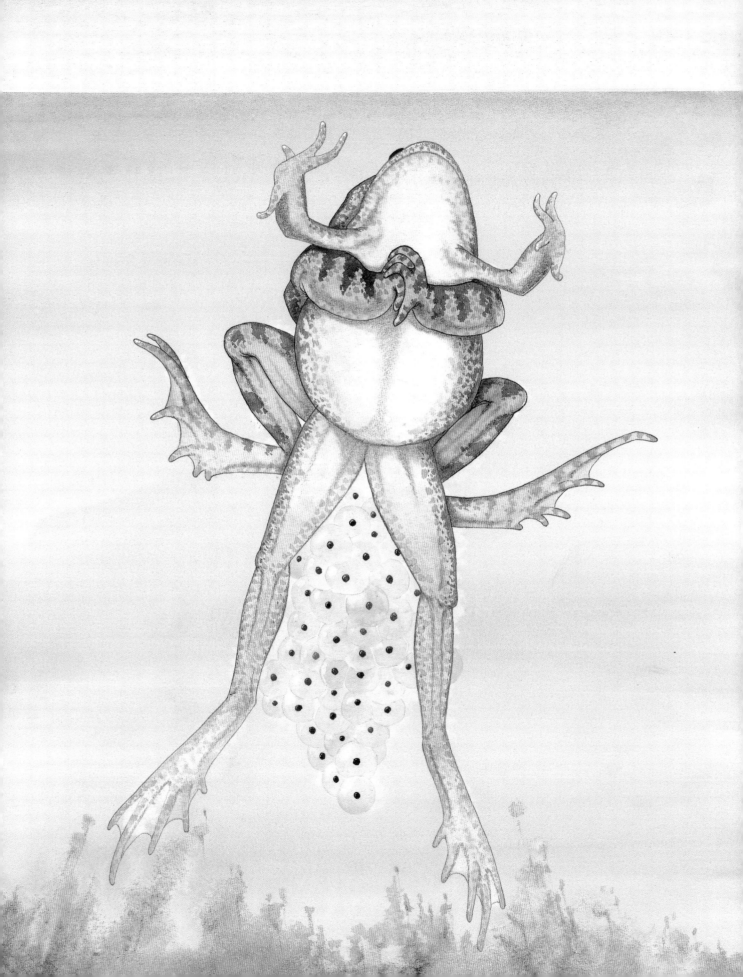

More about frogs

What is a frog?

A frog belongs to a group of animals called amphibians. Amphibians evolved from fish and can live on land and in water. Other types of amphibian include toads, newts and worm-like creatures called caecilians. Frogs have long back legs, webbed feet and no tail. Most frogs lay their eggs in water.

Where do frogs live?

There are more than 4,000 different kinds of frog, which live all over the world except in Antarctica. We often see the common or grass frog in Europe. The green frog and the bullfrog are common in North America. Many kinds of frog are becoming rare because of pollution, climate change and the destruction of the places where they live.

How big is a frog?

Common frogs and green frogs can be up to 10 cm long. The bullfrog is much bigger – up to 20 cm long. Most frogs are more active at night than in the daytime.

THE FROG IS A
POWERFUL JUMPER

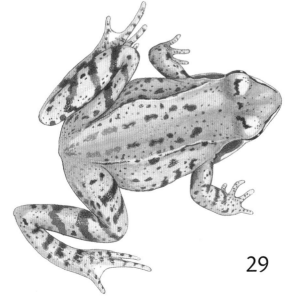

Words to remember

amphibian
An animal such as a frog or toad that can live
on land and in water.

fertilize
A male frog fertilizes eggs by releasing his sperm
in the water with the eggs. A fertilized egg can
grow into a frog.

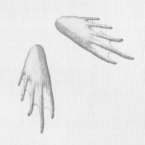

froglet
A tiny frog.

frogspawn
A frog's eggs.

gills
Parts of the body that help an animal breathe in water.

lungs
A part of the body used for breathing air.

prey
An animal that is hunted and eaten by another animal.

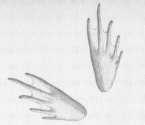

sperm
Cells from the male frog that join with the female's egg to make baby frogs.

survive
To stay alive.

tadpole
The first stage of the life of a frog.

webbed feet
Webbed feet have flaps of skin between the toes. This makes the feet into paddles that help the frog move in water.

Websites

All about frogs – lots of information about frogs
http://allaboutfrogs.org/

Frog information and pictures
www.arkive.org/common-frog/rana-temporaria/images.html

BBC factsheet
www.bbc.co.uk/nature/wildfacts/factfiles/483.shtml

Index